LAUGHTER
SAVED
MY CHILDHOOD SANITY

By Mick McNally

Editing, design, typesetting and publishing by UK Book Publishing.
www.ukbookpublishing.com

ISBN: 978-1-918077-02-5

Mick sadly passed away on 29th June 2025 before receiving a physical copy of his beloved book project. His sister Jane wanted to ensure his project was complete to bring his legacy to life.

"Knowing he picked the front cover and the book's blurb and authorising the content the last time I saw him and knowing how happy he was to have accomplished his dream helps come to terms with the loss of my big brother."

CHAPTER 1
CHILDHOOD FUN AND FEARS

We all look back with nostalgic memories. My first recollection was my mother saying "Michael, get down from those curtains, you will be letting the light out! The government has told everyone to keep them shut in case Germans fly over and drops bombs on us!"

"Why!" I asked.

"Because we are at war with Germany."

"What is war?" I asked.

"When people are killing one another," she replied.

"Why don't they stop then!" I said.

"When the man that started it all is dead!"

What an introduction to come into the world.

"The government gave us these gas masks, one for you and one for Doreen," my mother said. Doreen being my older sister.

They built a concrete air raid shelter on the patch at the end of the street – houses in those days had no carpets, just a peg rug in front of the fire or the bed. The warmest room was in the lounge, bedtime was hot water bottles and scraping the ice from inside the windows in the winter.

I started school in the Autumn of 1947. The coldest winter for many years; walkways had to be dug out of the snow along the pavements and I could not see over the top. "Go with your sister, just follow the children," I was told. Droves of them were making their way to school – in those days parents rarely escorted them to school. It was much safer in those days, I always smile when I hear the story, that the brilliant comedian Dave Allen tells of the first day he started school. With a huge creaking door and a nun waiting to meet him with a ruler in her hand. As a Catholic, I always thought religion was top of the agenda on my father's side. They were all devout Catholics but Mother thought they were a bunch of hypocrites; we suffered the difference of the orange and the green. The only orange she had sampled was in her gin. Hypocrites, she would say, drinking, fighting and committing every sin under the sun, then going to a half drunken priest to confess and ask for forgiveness. They are full of spirit alright! I have seen the brewery truck delivering barrels of beer to the priest house. One day a priest called around as she gave birth to the latest addition towards the 11 she ended up bringing into the world. Dad was a practising Catholic alright.

The priest said, "Those two children standing by the bed have not been Christened. God gave you the gift of those children." She glared at him and said, "Yes, and he has given me the bloody pain to go with it! You are full of spirits alright; I have seen the barrels being delivered to the priest house!"

Dad was in a panic and apologised, saying that she had been under stress of late. Not the fact that she has an uncontrollable temper and a split personality. One day she would be a broody hen with chicks and the next a bird of prey. Oh, how she could talk, I think she had been injected with a gramophone needle. Mainly all scandal about neighbours. She could argue with her own shadow. Dad hired a horse and cart,

2

and a set of harnesses – he was a street hawker selling fruit and veg, just after the war. He wore a rabbit skin coat in the winter that his dad had made him out of rabbit skin, from poached rabbits. Mother said, "It looks like a scruffy patchwork quilt." He said, "I don't care what I look like with the Northeast wind cutting up your coat in February!"

Years later my Uncle Jim used to say to his wife, when Steptoe and Son came on the TV, look there goes George with his horse and cart. But he made a living out of it for about 20 years. He did progress to an old truck – more about that later!

Reflecting on my childhood, seeing the funny side to things helped; as I said, my mother had a temper. My mate Alfie used to ask what mood she was in when he called for me. She did go over the top at times. When I was about three or four years old and misbehaved, she grabbed me by the scruff of the neck and threw me in the coal hole. It was small and pantry sized with no window. I used to feel my way along the wall to the hatch where the coal was tipped in and slip the bolt back and hear her say, "Are you going to behave yourself now? If so, I will open the door". I would be outside the kitchen door and would be sniggering to see the look on her face when she realised I'd got out. That stopped that punishment. Although, I think a lot of parents would give their kids a clip around the ear.

It was not pleasant in those times in cold houses, food rationing and queues everywhere. The rows were on a regular basis. I hated going to school or church. I recall a time when I was ten years old. We had what was called dancing lessons in the hall. There were more boys than girls, me and a couple of mates would hang back so we didn't have to dance with the girls as we thought it was for "sissys". So, we fooled around at the back of the hall. The class was taken by Miss Howell, a spinster, bun at the back of her head and parted in the middle. She would not look out of place as a prison guard. As I slid around the floor she pounced on me, grabbing my arms, and must have known I hated dancing and tried to turn me into Fred Astaire. But she could not move me; I thought of that song, I won't dance, don't ask me. Next second, she grabbed my hair like a Jack Russell on a rat, shaking it. I don't know how I held my fists back, but Dad always said, "Respect your elders! And don't bring trouble back here". I saved the hair to show my mother. She hit the roof. "I will skull drag the bitch!" she said. It is funny she would give me a good hiding, but nobody else could. She said, "Wait until I go to that school!" I was chuffed, looking forward to a front seat at the fight. But Dad stepped in. "I will go and sort it out," he said. DAMN!! I thought. It would have been been a better show if Mother had have gone.

Miss Howell was red from the neck up when he said, "I had to stop my wife coming around as she threatened to skull drag you." He told the school it's no problem giving him the cane!! "Thanks, Dad!" I thought. "BUT never grab hold of children's hair." The headmaster told my dad that Miss Howell had been under some stress of late. I know!! I felt it!!

Even on dinner duty, she would instruct the pupils to put down their utensils quietly after meals. I remember, my younger sister, who was about six years of age getting a smack to the back of her leg, for stacking her plate too loud. The shock on her little face. I had to hold myself back from punching her one (Miss Howell, that is). There was an old-fashioned saying…spare the rod and spoil the child. I agree if they deserved it, but she was sadistic.

I was never happier than when in the countryside. Those days when the air was full of birdsong. It seems every town was only a mile or two away from green fields or a wood. Even in the Black Country while it was full pelt with industry, there were always patches of rough ground or the odd coppice. Ponds full of frogs and newts and a good variety of birdlife. Now it is all under concrete. The outskirts of Wolverhampton, where I lived, you could see 20 different types of birds. Greenfinch, Chaffinch, Goldfinch, Larks, Yellowhammers, Wagtails, Partridges, Owls and bats, the list goes on. One of the most common was the song thrush, to be seen and heard on every street. Today, it is as good as extinct. I wrote a poem, called the last song thrush.

Boys like me had an egg collection in those days. It seems shocking now, but we were told it is OK to take one egg as long as there were three or more in the nest. One day I was out bird nesting with a couple of mates, Frankie and Dennis, over Bushbury Bonk and down to the black and white farm and into ten bob wood. I was high up a tree when a loud voice said, "Get down from that bloody tree!" There stood a well-built man in a gamekeeper's outfit, with a large shotgun over his arm. My mates just froze. He grabbed my tin of eggs and stamped on them and said, "If I see you little bastards again, I am going to shoot you!"

As he straightened the shotgun up, I heard a familiar sound coming from Frankie's trousers – he had shit himself. We never did go back there again. Most families had several children, and we had regular games, marbles, conkers and kick the can. In the winter we made slides on the ice, down the middle of the road. One extended over 40 yards long, I bet two dozen of us were sliding down it. I took off at full pelt and my legs shot from under me. I found myself looking up at faces looking down, I had stunned myself. In the night, some miserable sod had tipped a bucket of ash over it. Still, it was a danger to the old folk walking. One day, me and my mate saw for the first time on the estate a man with a brown face and a turban on his head. We had never seen anything like this except, Abu the elephant boy at the cinema. We did see a little girl with a brown face; her hair fascinated us. Her mother told the neighbours that her husband came home from the Middle East and had a dark tan. I heard my dad say, "Pull the other one!" So, we followed the brown man asking him questions. Did he have an elephant??

One of my mates said, "I hope you head gets better soon, mister." We didn't know any better in those days.

My word, when you compare how things have changed. It seems every man had a job; if someone was on state benefits, he would be called a scrounger. Mind you, there was a factory or workshop in every area. Still the workshop of the world. You could not even imagine how things have changed. The country was literally built on coal, every house had a coal fire in the winter. There was always a low fog when no wind was blowing. At about eight years of age, waiting in the queue in the coal yard with an old pram, pushing a bag of coke back for the fire. My teeth chattering when I got home. Horses were still being used on the odd occasion, by the bread man, and huge shire horses pulling brewery trucks with the barrels on, delivering to pubs. There were the rag and bone cart, brass trumpet and the yell of "Any old rags!" with his horse drawn cart.

I remember a mate of mine got dragged back down the road by his ear, by his mother. He had given the rag and bone man a bag of rags with his brother's jumper in it for a day-old chick. She said, "Wait 'til your father gets home from work!" On another day, I was playing with my pal Patrick, in his grandfather's garden. He said, "Watching you young boys enjoy yourself," with tears in his eyes, "I remember I was a happy young man not much older than you two. The government called all of us up and sent us over to France, to fight, it was horrible. A shell blew me up and crippled me. That is why I walk with a limp. So, if another one starts, don't go!! Let those who start it, fight it!" At that his wife said, "Roger, don't re-live it. World War One and World War Two are over!"

Dad always said stand up for yourself. If I had told him so-and-so hit me, he would take me back to fight them. I must smile, when I hear the old saying "Stand up to a bully they always back down". Now back to reality, they're usually bigger, stronger with a disposition like a pit bull with the piles and blacks your other eye!!

Reflecting back to school days, marching in line, you could hear a pin drop in class with some teachers. Dress was usually dark grey or black. One Christmas, an uncle from Canada sent us a present. Mine was a lumberjack jacket with big red and blue squares. It was fantastic and warm in the winter; the only snag was I had no change of clothes and had to go to school in it. I stood out like a Belisha beacon. I got sick of my mates shouting "TIMBER".

I always laugh and think of the best country and western singers, Dolly Parton, singing the coat of many colours my mamma made for me. She also sampled the hardships of being one of a big family. Her mother making a coat of many colours, she loved hers, but I felt like a technicoloured guppy and hated it. It reminded me of priests jabbering on in mass in Latin – you would kneel on hard benches with bony knees, along with half a dozen of us with tongues out waiting for the wafer, like a nest of young chaffinches. Swinging the incense around in all his splendour. Here is a quicky:

The Christian bows before the cross and fills you full of hope. But the one they followed long time back did not dress up like t he pope.

The Catholic church always preaches about the sins of wrongdoings, but it seems to me that the sins of the flesh were always at the top of the list. I remember a young 16-year-old girl got pregnant and was the talk of the town. A shameful sinner, so it seems that God sees all from his celestial throne in the sky. You seem to be living in fear from this Holy Joe, peeping Tom. I remember one day, as a ten-year old in class, getting what we call…a stalk on! As we called it. It would not go down, I prayed but the harder I prayed, the harder it got!! These days, I pray it will stand up! I remember a girl in my class saying "Giz a look!" I was brave enough to flash it if she showed me hers, which she did. The next morning, she said she was telling the teacher… "WHAT!!!"

She stood up with her hand in the air. I thought "you little bitch!". My heart was pounding. God, what would the teacher say. Stand in front of the class and then there was the priest and worst of all, my mother. But she went to the desk

8

and then out of the classroom, then came back grinning – she had only asked to leave the room. What a horrible cruel trick. I never got a stalk on for another month and kept well buttoned up!!

In those days there were no washing machines, just the tub and a dolly made, rubbing board and mangle. So, my younger brother and me, for the price of an ice-cream, would tread and jump on the washing in the bath full of soapy water. We had the cleanest feet in the street. Doing anything to make a bit of cash,. I asked Dad as he unharnessed the horse from the cart and took the horse back to the paddock, by the priest house – my price was a penny to pull the cart from the patch. It was about fifty yards downhill. He said I didn't ask you to do it and only gave a half penny. My mother said, "He'd skin a gnat for its eye!" So true.

I dug the back garden for two bob (or ten pence). I don't want to sound like a miserable old so-and-so but wish certain youths of today would sample what our generation sampled. To make them appreciate what a cushy life they have got. Looking back there was never much sentiment for most animals – they were all meat for the pot. I had a pet duckling and loved digging worms up and seeing it dash for them, to my amusement. Until it got to a good size and guess what was for Sunday dinner...

The one thing that really broke my heart was when I was about four years of age, Dad bought a little liver and white Spaniel puppy. I grew up with it as children do, I used to throw it sticks and stones but was told not to throw stones. When I went out for long walks and getting into ponds, she would come back the same as me, covered in mud.

Some years later, as she was a bitch, dogs would hang outside the door, at a certain time of the year. So, Mom said she had to go. Dad said he would find her a home on a farm or a distance away. Mom said, "No, she will find her way back, I want her put down." She had a cruel streak in her that was hard to understand, when she was in that state of mind and it caused me to be angry with my father for always giving in to her. So, if a dog lover gets a bit emotional about "Ol Shep", I can certainly understand them. I broke my heart as a nine-year-old and to hold hatred towards your mother is an odd emotion indeed, but we all act on our experiences.

I recall one situation when I helped Dad on his fruit and veg round, he hired a horse and cart, I don't know why it came with a leather muzzle. He must have been mistreated in the past – if anybody walked too close, he would flatten his ears and sometimes hear his teeth snap in the muzzle. One day, a guy said, "I'm used to horses" and went to pet him on the head and it bit him on the chest. Then a familiar sound echoed on the street on the estate where we lived, called The Scotlands. Named after poets, like Dickens and Keats. It had a bit of a reputation for some unsavoury characters. They mostly worked in those days; well the sound reverberated down the street was the brass band of the Salvation Army. Followed by scores of kids. At that, Billy, the horse, started to dance in the shafts. Dad said he was about to bolt. "Hold onto his head, while I ask the bandmaster to stop playing."

"You hold mad Billy!" I replied.

He agreed. "I will ask the bandmaster to stop playing." The band walked by in silence; what a relief. I took the easy way out; he did bolt once before when a box dropped to the back of his legs and apples bounced off the cart. Kids ran in the street, and dashed in gateways and out again to stay clear, but when he ran past, they started grabbing all the apples. Dad said, "There goes all the profits." Also, in those days there was a pair of police houses on every estate. One copper with his short, cropped hair, a heavyweight who looked like he done a fair few rounds. He stood no nonsense, with discipline, like a clip around the ear. If ever he heard us calling him the nickname the boys gave him – "Crabface the Copper" – he would get on his bike and chase you for miles.

I once got a ride on a policeman's bike at six years of age. My mother said, "Stand by the gate while I go to the shops." She was a late riser. Dad used to tell us to be quiet and take her a newspaper and a cup of tea to keep her in bed. To give our ears a rest, first thing in a morning. Anyway, in the six-weeks school holiday we were up at six am with the sun shining, and by about 10 o'clock in the morning, whilst she was having a lie in we still hadn't had any breakfast. So, I decided to follow her the other way around, down to the shops instead of doing as I had been told, and got lost. A man called the policeman who said, "Don't worry, son, we will soon find where you live. Jump on the crossbar of my pushbike," and pedalled me to the Heath Town police station. He asked if I was hungry, and I said "Yes". He said, "Here have a couple of sandwiches." I scoffed them. "Well, you soon got through them, here have the other two, my Mrs will do some more."

About half an hour later, Dad arrived to pick me up. The copper said, "You want to feed the kid, he is famished." My mother got it in the neck when Dad got back. She said, "He should have done as he was told and waited by the gate." I thought coppers are not so bad after all. I entered this little episode to reflect how parents were in those days. They would say take a couple of jam sandwiches and go to the park. You may not return until five pm so off we would go with a couple of friends.

My mother always had a bit of a "Mrs Bucket" attitude from Keeping Up Appearances. Never spoke with a Black Country accent and thought it was common, she dressed well and looked down a lot on folk, saying they were uncouth. She was an attractive woman in her youth, but I would prefer a plain Jane who didn't nag so much and fly off the deep end for nothing. One night, after catching the late bus packed with the Scotlands mob, as she called them, a woman with a Black Country accent said, "Ay yow Mrs Mac the Tater Mon's Mrs?" This ruffled her feathers right up. "Bloody Scotlands' mob," she said.

The house move was great, especially to my mother – it was a house with a field in front and a golf course backed onto it. With the sewage works up the road and a canal. But much better than living on a council estate. In the summer the sound of birdsong. The one big setback was it was built of concrete. No cavity walls and a real fridge in the winter. Concrtete floors and stairs, when you get out of bed, it was two leaps down the stairs, no pyjamas, just a long vest pulled down to your knees. Jockeying for position by an open fire. With five others. I never forgot one cold winter's morning when the back boiler exploded due to frozen water pipes, supplying water to the boiler. It exploded like a bomb, chunks of cast iron made holes in the ceiling. It was a good job it was the top of the boiler and not the front. Mother and two sisters needed hospital treatment, Josie was the baby and in a split second after the explosion the room went pitch black with soot and stream and scattered hot coals across the floor. Dad had to feel around the floor for the baby. It was that dark, she had burns to her legs and thighs off the hot coals. I got away with a few lumps and bumps and a black soot-splattered face. I was so lucky; I was bending warming my backside. Otherwise, I would not be writing this today. My other brother was also lucky to not be injured as iron shrapnel hit the wall near where he was standing. Eight of us in a 16-metre square room. Next day it was off to school as normal, what an excuse to have a day off. "But Dad, I have shell shock!" "No, Mick" he said, there is a hole in the wall where the fire was and no fire, it is not worth a day off. "Damn, these days I would be spoon fed ice-cream in hospital by a hot nurse!" How times have changed. To cut a long story short, Dad received payment for the burnt carpet and sofa. But in those days, there was no legal aid, to sue the council for personal damage and shock for injuries received. Due to lack of proper insulation around the water pipes. His brother, Uncle Jim, offered to lend him the money to sue the council but he declined the offer. Well, the good old days, I think some children of today complain about next to nothing. I am the oldest boy of eleven, but my sister Doreen is about 18 months older; our task was to babysit while our parents went out of a night. On other occasions on having a new arrival about every 18 months, it was non-stop – even today, I can't stand the sound of a baby grizzling and crying. When you have about ten years of shift work, and rocking and changing them or a hot neck whilst one sits on your neck to amuse them, then it gets a bit too much. The comedian Les Dawson reminds me when he said we had that many nappies in the bathroom we had a rainbow in the kitchen. I never married or had children – I served my time with them during my childhood. I chose adventure instead. From Tabletop Mountain in South Africa to the Blue Mountains of New South Wales, and the outback of Lightning Ridge opal fields, mining. I had quite a few adventures in my life and not forgetting a few romances with the fairer sex.

Going back to living in a concrete ice box. Next door was an old widower, he used to cut his own hedge at 90 years of age and seemed to always be putting bags on his Dahlias. After he passed away, one summer's day we heard a loud commotion coming down the road. It was a big flat truck, backfiring and chugging along, it was loaded high with furniture, tied on with rope, about eight kids on the top. Our tranquillity had gone. The Preeces had arrived, they arrived like the Beverly Hillbillies. They turned out OK once we go to know them. I remember me and Billy Preece, the second oldest, used to go for a swim in the cut on a hot summer's day. His younger brother was always into mischief – one day he almost hung his younger brother. They made a swing on the oak tree and the noose slipped around his neck and Bill had to cut him down. One day I heard shouting and doors slamming, and out flew Stan the mischievous one, with Bill on his tail. His mother shouting, "Give it to him, Bill". That means a thumping. He had eaten all the bread; he was always in trouble, a real daredevil. He'd climbed the highest tree and swam back from a swan's nest with an egg in his trunks. While they dive bombed him under the water. One day, my younger brother George and Stan went out into the countryside, with another mate about 12 years old. Came back with a large dead cockerel each under their coats. My brother and Stan got a good dressing down – they said, but they were all running loose. Both fathers decided that the only thing to do, was to eat the evidence. Stan's father saw active service in the Middle East, and he did say it gave many a man a good home, so one day when young Stan was around 17 years of age, and his dad waiting to reprimand his for some misdemeanour he had committed, he said, "Dad, I have took the King's Shilling". So, instead of getting it in the neck, he took him for a pint. The barman said, he isn't old enough and his dad said, "Pour him a bloody pint. I played my part in the war and look what we came back to, rationing and poverty". He got his pint. In fact, Stan continued his mischievous deeds whilst serving in the army. In fact, he made the newspaper – somehow, he had purchased an old cannon and having access to gunpowder he decided to drill out the sealed-up hole that the powder was applied to but as he told me it would only go pop. So, I packed it with a larger amount of powder and fixed a fuse and stood back, then the shed disintegrated.

It was said to be heard a mile away. The newspaper stated, Stan blows up shed. I met him in Queensland Australia, for I stayed with him. He also saw active service and marched and marched with the ANZACS each year. Speaking of dangerous situations, this tale makes me laugh every time I think about it. When I was about 13 years of age, trimming cabbages, as we lived near the canal, old Sammy Lomas, the lock keeper, said "Son, bring the leaves back for my hens, and I will give you a shilling." He then proceeded to tell me about the time that the Germans tried to bomb Doughty Bolten and Paul's aircraft factory; he said, "When I drained the cut, I found a bomb. I struggled to get it out, it weighed a tonne. I put it in an old pram and pushed it to a local police station". He said, "I shouted 'Hey, Sarge, come and see what I found in the cut'!" He pulled the cover off it and the Seargeant said, "Get that fucking thing out of here!!"

Another event regarding the next-door neighbour. She was very concerned and explained that her sister who was visiting her, that both of them being pensioners, she said, "Elsie, I have got a gas leak. Can you smell it?" "Yes" she said. "Where is the gas meter?" "Oh, it is down the cellar, but I ain't got a light down there." "Hang on a bit, I will go and light a candle," she said. We both got to the bottom of the steps and screamed and ran back up.

Well, by the time I was 11, Dad had progressed to an old truck; not saying it was a big improvement to being outside, in the winter, holes in the floor, no such thing as a heater. I often thought of the milkmen, with electric vehicles with no doors on. I think you needed to be a cross between a polar bear and a human to work in one of those all day.

Saturday, we worked from eight am after loading the truck until ten pm, and Sunday eight am until two pm. For two shilling and all the fruit you could eat. I remember digging the back garden, for just two shilling, but still I preferred to be outside earning a bit to sitting in a classroom, bored out of my brain. Who gives a toss what king overthrew who in the Middle Ages or discover what is the capital of Venezuela, or naming the continents. Most of us pupils were what was described as factory or cannon fodder. OK, bricky, plasterer or mechanic today. I honestly believe once you have learned reading, writing and arithmetic at the age of 12 the next following years, nothing can be added. I believe to us working class boys. I hated the unbelievable repetitive nature of it, especially the winter's journey. Travelling through hail, rain and snow. Walk half a mile to the bus stop, two-mile journey on the bus then walk another mile. When I first arrived at senior school, they were just finishing a toilet block. Being a Catholic school, I think it was being underfunded and the previous block, so to speak, was an open trough with water constantly running along the length of the building, right under the cubicles, no flush chains; some pupils used to try and light paper and float it if a pal was sitting doing his business. The school was called St Joseph's, the headmaster was a Mr Morgan. About 5ft 3 inches, a proper Arther Askey of a figure. He would have loved to have trod the boards of the old hall theatre, I am sure. At the school assembly, he would be congratulating the boxing team, for another win. We had the best boxing team in Wolverhampton, out of the schools. He would then give us a treat, his rendition of "I've got sixpence a jolly jolly sixpence" and "These old lavender trousers". I reckon they were a hit during the Boer War, mind you, he could give you a few lashings of the cane and say, "Boy, this hurts me more than it hurts you". One day a pupil got a dose of the cane and passed out. He said drag him off, well not quite in that manner. While addressing the school's boxing team's success, one boy put his hand up. But you don't interrupt him while he has got the floor. He was speaking of a famous, bare-knuckle fighter, called the Tipton Slasher of the past. "What is it, boy?" he growled. "Please sir, the Tipton Slasher was my Grandad." The hall erupted in laughter. He said, "Are you in the boxing team, Perry?" He said, "No, Sir". Looking at the boxing instructor, Mr Morgan said "put his name down". Perry swallowed hard and wished he hadn't put his hand up. There was one school which always beat us though and that was called Rowley Regis, and we were due to box them that night. When into our area stepped a little banty cock, like me, more meat on a butcher's knife. "Who is McNally?" my competitor said. I replied, "Me". He said, "Well I am going to murder you and give you a right good ommering!" There is nothing like confidence. Well, I lasted the distance, I think the word is psyching you up. A pal of mine turned out to be a good boxer, Peter Davis. We were pals from infant school, I can remember gardening when another pupil, Phillip, tried to skim his foot with a gardening fork and it went through his foot. Many years later I worked on a building site as we were both plasterers, he told me I meant to skim his foot; also when Peter became a good boxer at senior school and needed a sparring partner, he would send for Phillip. He said my bloody nose was so sore he gave me during those sessions I think it was revenge for his foot.

One day Pete showed up on a tandem bike. "Fancy biking to Bridgenorth?" It was 14 miles away. We had great fun, racing the bus back, each time it stopped we overtook it, to the amusement of the passengers. Thirteen-year-old legs going round like catherine wheels, but of course it was only one car every half hour in those days.

In the six weeks school holiday we went camping for a couple of nights. You could not camp out on the common without a warning to be gone next morning. Miserable morons, give them a badge and a pen, and they swell up. I recall the last day at school in the assembly hall, all the staff and headmaster wishing us pupils a final farewell and good luck. After four years of earbashing. History and religious lessons, totally worthless to us pupils, who would only remain manual workers. I thought then as I think now, it is all for indoctrination. Don't question it, just take the orders.

In 1957 it was a time of Elvis and Bill Hayley, and a classroom mate was the comic of the class; he saved all his paper round money and spent it on a Teddy Boy outfit, blue jacket, black velvet collar, drainpipe trousers and brothel creepers on his feet. Mr Morgan's eyes narrowed as he investigated the class of school leavers. "Leighton, come here and get on the stage. What the hell do you think you are wearing; you are inappropriately dressed for school. Bend over that desk." He lifted his longtail coat up and gave him some lashes with his cane across his backside. The mean arrogant bastard couldn't resist to demonstrate the attitude of "I am still in charge" with just ten minutes to go for school leavers. The look of disgust that came over our class as Bunny took the punishment. We called him that, his name was Bernard and hated being called Bunny; he was a very popular boy and didn't deserve that. Leaving school was one of the happiest days of my life at the age of 15. No more four-mile journeys, through hail, sleet and snow only to be bored half to death, with a new style of maths, Pythagoras's theory etc. I was about to launch into my new role, following my dad's line as a street hawker, of fruit and veg. I first bought a horse drawn metal milk float, two small wheels at the front, like three-wheeler Robin Reliant, it cost a fiver. Next for a horse's set of harness, you could hire a horse and cart and a set of harness in the Black Country, for a quid a week.

So, I went to Horace Cox to hire a horse, old Horace came out with a Black Mare about 14-2 – "she's a good mare but sometimes she gets a bit spooky. Especially if there is a trolley bus about. Now mount up, I will cycle alongside you, to get you started". I had only sat on a horse once before. I started what is called clicking her. You know when you call a dog with your tongue. But instead of coming they are going. The more I clicked the more it trotted. I thought I clicked to slow her down, but now she was cantering with old Horace Cox, pedalling like mad and foaming at the mouth. Shouting, "Stop, clicking her, stop clicking her!!!. Dow click 'er it meks um guw faster!!" I finally got the message and felt more confident, like a bit of a cowboy. I loved Westerns then. Nearing a shopping centre a trolley bus went by, with the overhead wires clicking. Suddenly, she began to dance, I shifted all over the place, onto the pavement, scattering all the shoppers. Talk about dance, I thought I was on Michael Flatley's shoulders. She soon settled down into a paddock with about 20 other horses. It was what was referred to as a horse riding stables. It was run by a Mr Bill West, six foot tall, six teeth and a woodbine permanently hanging from his mouth. Let's face it, smoking was good for you in those days. The next one I have will be my first. You would smell like a smoked kipper. If you went to a football match, or a pub, which I never did, I think I can remember remnants of four old farms around Wolverhampton. Due to the expanding population. Housing estates were springing up everywhere, covering the greenery. Mind you, I remember the decaying old rows of slums with terraced houses and outside brew house, with a tin bath in for a bathroom. Most certainly after going through World War Two, I think if they did not change the system, what with food rationing and the means test, you had to sell everything in the house, except a table, a couple of chairs and a bed, leaving you only a few items, that you were eligible for a small pittance. I dare not go on about today's system or I would blow a gasket. I think between the age of 15 and 18 was our best days. There was a crowd of about 20 youths of us, teenagers, galloping along the bridle paths between farmland and up along the long grass verges on some roads with very little traffic. We used to collect all the grass, along the verges and Bill towed his trailer, we would collect all the cut grass, would you believe, along the centre of the Stafford Road in Coven on a quiet Sunday morning. I think there was about one car every half an hour and now it is about a thousand an hour. There was always frolicking in the hay loft with the girls, with Bill shouting, "Get down from the hay loft. Do your courting outside the gates!!" Mind you, I can remember at least four couples who got married, that in early times rolled in the hay. One day I said to Bill, "Why do you call that horse Beauty? He has a bucket-like head, sway back and a scruffy coat." Bill said, "Look again." His fifth leg was hanging in the short grass, that is how he got his name.

So, my attempt to make a living as a street hawker was a disaster, you can't grab a customer by the neck and say, "Come and buy my fruit". One day Dad said, "You are spending, more time galloping the shoes off that horse around the bridle paths." He was right I just wanted to be a cowboy instead. I loved early Westerns, like Sugar foot and The Cisco Kid and The Lone Ranger. He was so gay, he fired solid silver bullets and when he put on that mask, all of it, two inches across, no one had a clue who he was.

Fast forward three years, after getting a variety of jobs, it was it don't matter what you do, if you pay your board. My mother would say "We've kept you long enough, go and earn some money." When I first left school, I could not take on an apprenticeship, with just thirty bob a week, that was about £1.50. That won't keep you, go and earn some money. So, I delivered milk and coal and a touch of window cleaning, and a driver's mate to Knackermon Ned, which inspired one of my Black Country poems.

It was the smelliest job in town, a sausage skin factory, animal waste material for fertilizer. Fred drove a truck around, with about sixty bins on the back, he had a contract, collecting all the animal intestines and by-products from butchers' and slaughterhouses. When I first started I was just throwing the bins on in any fashion. He shouted, "NO, No!!" Every bin has its place on the truck for loading and unloading. My job was on the truck with a metre long bar, with a handle on the top and a hook on the bottom. One, two, three and UP!!

Some weighed about a couple of hundred pounds, of course with blood and other liquids in them they had to be lowered rather than dropped. I got a bollocking from Fred one day because he had red and brown freckles through me dropping the bin a bit heavy. He was a very conscientious worker; I believe he had shares in the firm. He used to say, "My name in Kneller," he added, "it is German with a K." I felt some of the men thought he was a bit of a know-it-all. We had what was called a snap cabin, a room for eating your midday sandwiches. There were two tables we used for card games. Of course, there is a lot of characters; one worked in a tiny room, salting the bladders for different meats, his name was Walter, so of course it was Walter the salter. There was a lot of different comments and opinions across the workforce.

As in many work situations and much mickey taking. Fred was in the old-time boxing association; he used to give me a gummy smile and say "Nothing false about me!". Some of the men thought Fred with a German name was bit of a know-it-all. Well, we all wore wellies and overalls. The boys would say what sort of a day with Kneller as they called him. I said, "I have had a very difficult day today, because he has been goose stepping in his wellies again." The men just howled.

One day someone was talking about poison, that bacteria, called salmonella. I said as I always made a comment about mispronunciations, what a mouthful. I said I thought salmonella was Fred's brother, but what I did not know was he did have a brother named Sam. They had a good laugh. Fred said, "Poison, he ain't far off as he never got on with his brother."

Come 18, a knock on our door, and Dad said, "It is Uncle Matt." That was his brother, and he is starting a job on a new school, as a general labourer – "do you want a job? It's a tenner a week for five and half days, plus a bonus". Uncle Matt was stranded on Dunkirk along with thousands. He said we all had the Maltese Cross on the beach, flat on your face, flattened in the sand as much as we could. While that fat bastard Goring's Stucker continued to strife us! Was I glad to get on that boat. It sounds strange, £10 a week, while today it is £20 an hour. Plus, no money if you stopped for rain. It is an education, all the different characters you come across in different workplaces. Some were comedians, some sarcastic bullies, enjoying taking the pee out of you. Big Bert, a six-foot strapping brickie, said to the young apprentice, "Yow om a Vergin aye ya!" He looked back nervously at Big Bert and said, "I have kissed a couple of girls." "I know you were a virgin," grins Bert. This goes on, for some time, weeks later the apprentice said, "I have got a girlfriend." "But yowm still a virgin." Bert nods. Next day the apprentice said, "I have took your advice and I am no longer a virgin." Each morning Bert would ask inappropriate questions to belittle the apprentice. One day he answered, "Yes, three times last night and she asked me to meet her parents tomorrow night." Well, the very next morning, as the boys were waiting to hear the banter, one asked, "Did you meet her parents?" He sheepishly looked at a very sad looking Bert and said "Yes".

You learn a lot on the building trade, you are deciding what you may take up. My next job was a hod carrier – a brickie's labourer: £16 for five and half days. Most small sites in those days had a hole dug in the ground and a plank rigged up with four corrugated steel sheets around to form a toilet. The hod was an implement for putting usually ten bricks in it, some of those old bricks weighed about three kilos. Up onto your shoulder and up the ladder, like a monkey with a stick, all day. It must have weighed about 30 kilos. You also mixed compo as it was called to lay the bricks. We used lime in the mix, not very nice on a windy day. Throwing it in the mixer with sand and cement. This caused cracked fingers. I remember not being used to it, and had only three fingers free of cracks. I carried and mixed all the bricks and mortar, that is a pair of semi-detached houses every three and half weeks, for nearly two years. It worked out a pair built by labour was around £250 – you could not dream the cost of a house today. The cost of buying a house was approximately £3,000.00. I disliked having to work in the rain, so I decided to go for another trade with an inside job. A plasterer's labourer, all hand mixed, you drop a hundred weight bag into a tin bath, making sure you stand the other side of the wind, mixing for two. One tonne a day, next day they would put the topcoat on, you used a six-gallon bucket with a length of roof lathe, with a bike cog welded on a metal rod and go up and down, until it creamed just right. I did what a lot of labourers do, and used the tools – I think one advantage of the building trade and not like factory conditions, especially during the summer months.

One old plasterer I used to work with on a red-hot day. "It is enough to make you want to strike your Granny. The first pint in the pub tonight will not touch my sides."

When a truck load of plaster arrived you would get five shilling a tonne for unloading, though you rarely got it off some of the slick operators, if you didn't watch it. Some building sites' safety and conditions were overlooked. I saw several accidents when we plastered the ceiling above the landing – we used to nail a piece of three by two across an upright plank that stood inside the stairwell and rested another plank from the landing onto a two inch wide, so you are working above your head with a razor sharp trowel while the plank you are standing on is just two inches wide.

Once, I saw the cable hoist that operates outside a block of flats come flying down, there was half a tonne the limit. I remember a couple of plasterers, one unloaded half the tonne, while his mate stood, about ten floors up, as it reached the level, I was behind him. He just started to slide the door open. There was a loud crack, the cable snapped, and it went screaming down to the ground with a big cloud of plaster dust as it hit the bottom. I realised that if you supplied the material as well as the labour, but still you had to outlay your money. I got into partnership with a guy called Brian. I admit I hated the bloody job, looking at bare walls all day, plastering them, day in day out, bitter cold wind in mid-winter, no glass in a lot of buildings and ruling off with a metal featheredge. Wet the spot board to put plaster and it turns to a sheet of thin ice first thing of a morning. I remember one job it was a bitter cold wind, no glass and a concrete floor. I said, "Bugger it, Brian, I have had enough of this job." He said, "It's ok if you are single, I would if I could I'd take a bit of time off in the winter." I could not understand how if I had a wife and two children it was not just physical but psychological. There was a big wide world out there to be discovered. Not looking at bare brick walls all day. When I watched Westerns in colour, how it uplifted me. Wide landscapes and endless blue skies, not rows and rows of terraced houses, and heavy industry was booming, still in the Black Country. The folk were the salt of the earth and accepted their fate, and proud of their hard, dirty schools. How they had been stabbed in the back by both sides of politics. OOHHPS I'm getting carried away. I have some observations to make but it would not be allowed to print. So, now in 1969 immediately after Enoch got sacked, so it is off to Down Under as a £10 Pome. I caught the train to Southampton docks. The folk in the cabin looked a bit on the posh side. When the conductor came around, he said "your carriage is three cars down". The toffee nosed so-and-so. So, I stepped in and said to a motley crew of passengers, "Is this the cattle truck for Australia?" and got a few chuckles. What a sight at the Southampton docks as I stood on a crowded deck – there were streams of ribbons from the dock to the ship. Tears fell like rain, for not seeing their kinfolk for years. Or even ever again. When suddenly the ship's hooter blasted, and the band struck up with life on the ocean waves. It slowly started away from the dock – my mother was there but she could not wave. Not because of sentiment, she had a pole in her arms to help the ship disembark. Well, we never did get on. It was great experience on what I regard as a luxury liner called The Northern Star. There were a couple of Brummie lads on and a farming family from Wellington, different folk from different parts of the world. Aussies, Kiwis and South Africans, as it was due to dock in Cape Town on its way to Australia. I made friends with a South African guy, a big strapping lad called George Pretorius. I said ain't that the capital of South Africa, he said yes it was named after a distant Boer War general, a relative of mine, he said. I love your humour, why don't you disembark in Cape Town instead of Australia? He said you will oversee a team of black workers on the building sites, instead of being on the tools. I must admit, I was tempted to jump ship. But the draw to the Aussie outback, as vast as it is, it was a bigger draw. I sat on the meal table with an OAP from Lancashire, her looks and accent reminded me of Gracie Fields, she was full of joy to be visiting one daughter in Aussie and one in New Zealand. She said it is all paid for by my daughters, I have not seen them for about 20 years. I thought it was quite touching. Then we had an ex-member of the crew, a bit posh, somehow at mealtimes he always had his sweet after dinner piled high. I commented this to Dolly the Lancashire lass, she said switch them. In an instant he knew and said you switched the desserts I paid extra for that. The toffee-nosed git. The fourth person was a cockney girl who said her name was Pratt with a double "t"; she was pig-sick about the weeks it took to reach our destination. We were all excited that we were disembarking in Sydney the next day. Everyone was looking forward to it but guess what? There was a strike on so off we sailed for another day. When you arrived, you were driven to a hostel and given a week of accommodation. It was a building with a passageway and rooms to accommodate four to a room. In two bunk beds. I was pleased to have a roommate, a young bricklayer about the same age. We hit it off straight away, he was from Yorkshire. We had a few jars of amber nectar together, we certainly needed it to get to sleep. There was a middle-aged guy who reached the Olympic final for snoring. I swear with his intake of breath he levitated off the bed. The other guy was as gay as a Christmas tree. He wore a hat like Dick Emery and suggested that me and Frank and himself rent a flat together. Well not being mean but the only visitors we wanted to our flat would be in a dress and not trousers. So, we found a place to rent, a large house with rooms and shared bathroom and kitchen and some Sheilas in the other rooms. The only snag, there was just one bed. I have never shared my bed before with a rough-arsed brickie. But we both agreed to point in opposite directions, plus we had fun with the girls. In 1969 the papers were full of ads for plasterers, brickies and carpenters etc. Scores of them every day, it was booming. Leave a job at 10am and at 2pm you could start another job. I hated the plastering trade even more because instead of internal plasterer, Gyprock, as we used to call it, but all the walls in Aussie were cement rendered and once more the Italians in cement work monopolised a lot of the trade. I was talking to a real dyed in the wool old

Aussie plasterer on the site. He said, "The bloody Dagos have ruined the trade and cut the prices, worse than the Pomes." I said, "Hang on, it was the Pomes that made Australia, the word POME is Prisoner of Mother England and these poor sods were the ones that toiled in the hot sun from morning until night laying the roads and building the first settlements, so in fact they were the champs not the chumps." He said, "Bollocks."

One of my first job was plastering swimming pools, the only snag was rising at 5am to beat the heat of the sun; the material was white waterproof cement and we had to finish the bowl in one go, in midday before it reached 38 degrees. Then it was time for a cold one. On another job it had hammered down with rain in the night, so me and Alan, the guy I was working for, started plastering the walls. The labourer had put a pump inside the pool with pipes extracting the water from the deep end. As I moved around the next minute, I was on my knees and blood pouring from a split head. He had only put a heavy brick to hold the pipe in place. Thank goodness it only dropped about half a metre. So, off to the hospital to get stitched up, I have never had such a hangover in my life. I started another job, this time it was for finishing plaster that I was used to. I met a guy who was a young German, we worked as a pair, his name was Wally, he said after the War he was shipped out to Australia like many youngsters from Germany and the rest of Europe and exploited as cheap labour. He said he was put to work on various outback jobs and a sheep station. He said at the age of 18 and ready to head for the big city lights, he said he had never had a woman and was still a virgin, so I made my way to King's Cross as I was told that women of the night frequent there. He said I went to a room where a scantily dressed woman said give me $20 and get undressed by the bed. He said just as I was folding my trousers up a big burly copper said get dressed you're coming with me – and I got fined another $20 and am still a virgin.

I sponsored a young brother out to Australia and moved into a flat near the sea. A big ten-storey block. There were still some mates living there from Wolverhampton, we called it cockroach castle, on account that it was built in the 50s and a lot of cavities in the internal walls were a perfect breeding place. When you came home late and switched on the light it resembled the African savannah. With herds of wildebeest and zebras heading for the walls. Aussie TV was total rubbish in those days, but the only show, it was so bad it was good, was an Australian talent show. Anyone could enter, I think they dragged them off the street, some played spoons, anything, we could not get in fast enough to watch it. The guy that ran the scoring resembled Sir Les Patterson. With a white suit, he was brutal, mind you, but was telling the truth. He said to one guy you are so bad; I could give you minus points. To which the singer said, right, mate, you are from Queensland, go back and shove your bananas up. Live on TV. It was great, it was real Aussie etiquette. It was a show that Paul Hogan first appeared on, he gave the arrogant panel a piece of his mind and said you can shove your points, I don't need them, I know I am good. The audience loved him, we all did. That is how he got started. Being by the sea was a great place to cool off, after a hard day's work. It was a little bay called Bronte. The first time I entered the surf, it was great. After a while, bells started ringing – as there were lots going on I thought it was a signal for an event or something. It must be good as all the bathers were leaving the sea. I was merrily enjoying the surf but asked about the last guy getting out, what was the event. Oh, he said, it is the shark alarm, next second, I was on the hot sand. Then came a building strike – there had been a few that year. I thought damn it, I always wanted to go to the huge outback, so I read about a place called Lightning Ridge, where you can find the most valuable black opal in the world. And could stake a claim for $5. Wow, that is for me, a huge landscape like being in a Western, so I bought a small generator and a Kango drill and headed five hundred miles inland. I did not see any Roos on the way, besides they are mainly nocturnal, but saw flocks of budgerigars, they are all green in the wild. The first guy we met was a scouser from Liverpool. He said, "I once played my squeezy box in The Tavern, where the Beatles sang." Within another day we met another guy, proper Aussie looking, bush hat, shorts etc, he said, "How Yow Gooing, our kid!" Bloody 'ell, you can't escape, he was from Dudley. "Yow cor lend us 10 bucks, can ya? I'm goin' through a bad patch at the minute but coming onto some good-looking ground. But I never got my ten bucks back, there were all nationalities trying their luck, but I am not talking about digging one metre down, its more like ten metres. Once more you blast your way down called shin cracker rock. The laid back attitude of the Aussie in those days was in the store near the Diggers' Rest pub, where I enquired about purchasing some gelignite. How many sticks are you looking for? He said, plonking a bundle on the counter like sticks of rock. Don't panic it won't go off; you can hit it, kick it or light it, it still won't go off without a detonator. And bullets, no problems, what sort do you want? Long nose

22 for a rifle. But it is funny with all the snakes and critters the worse thing of the lot was the blood sucking mosquitos. We timed it wrong after heavy rain, that filled old shafts with water a breeding ground for them. Me and the brother was nearly eaten alive. They came in clouds, I wrote a poem about them called **Enoch's Elderado**. But then everything bites you, red ants, black ants, green ants and the worst of all, I do not know the name of this one, but I parked my van next to a nest, I will call them Bulldog Ants, the description is about an inch and a quarter long, red legs and black body. I was just sipping my first cup of tea in the tranquillity of the early morning sunrise and listening to the magpies. Being an animal lover, I saw these large ants and sprinkled some sugar by them, not knowing these bastards were savages. I felt something like a red-hot poker on my bare foot and to see an ant bent over double, shoving his sting in as far as he could go. After I got off the roof of my van, I marinated him no more sugar for these outback savages. The blasting was necessary to sink the shafts to go through what is called Shin Cracker, about one metre of the 28 feet you go down, the rest was sandstone. All that was done with pick and shovel, we could bottom a shaft in about seven days, you had to check for anyone, close by when you were blasting, and get behind a big box tree. I kept the gelignite in a bag under my bed in the tent. I only found out it was the worst thing to do, as the polythene makes it sweat and turns it into nitro-glycerine. That will make it go off with a bang!! Do not believe what they show you on TV, it is damn hard to survive and just get your grub money. Occasionally you can get the odd snake fall down the shaft and perhaps live for a couple of years on frogs or other vertebrae that fall

down. There was always a bit of POME and Aussie banter, between us. Jim, an Aussie, was terrified of snakes. One day, as I was working in his mine, I saw a snake moving beneath the loose spoil, so I dispatched it with my pick and walked behind Jim holding the dead snake, level with his face and tapped him on the shoulder, and said what sort of snake is this? He nearly had a fit and called me a POME bastard! I used to go out with a rifle and shoot an odd rabbit or pigeon for a meal. One day I shot a wild boar, meaning a feral hog about 200 kilos. The reason I shot him was that they target the young lambs and eat them. I never shot for sport, so off I went with my rifle and compass, the dirt track about 20 miles long, I knew if I headed south, I would hit it if I went off track. So, into the bush, I went into the bush much further that I had been before. When I thought I was on my way back, it was a strange country, this is one area you do not want to get lost in is called the Malga Scrub, you'd never get out. The sun was getting lower, and I heard an explosion which came from a mining camp – I was headed in the wrong direction, the opposite direction. I was concerned if I got bitten by a snake, I could not get back in time. As the sun was low on the horizon, I came across a sheep shearing shed and followed a track up to a sheep station. Greeted by five barking dogs, was I glad to see a puzzled looking roust about. I said I had been lost for several hours; I asked for a drink of water. He said you are the first POME that has walked my 10,000 acres. He asked where I was from, I said the seven-mile camp. He said I am due to have a schooner in the Digger's Rest and will drop you off. I think he was grateful, because I rolled one of his ewes off her back in a paddock. What happens, is they are carrying a heavy fleece and roll on their back and can't get back to standing. They just die in the sun, or a wild boar comes along. Did they laugh? Where have you bloody been, they said in the camp. We set a charge off when we thought you might have got lost. I heard it, I said, I realised that the needle on the compass is magnetic and as I set my bearings off it was next to a metal tool, which attracted the needle. I won't watch my favourite old western again, The Big Country, because Peck did not get lost, he got his bearings right. So, from then on, it was tying a string to your belt, if you go into the bush for a crap!!

There are all sorts of crazy characters and a few dodging the law, one or two sleeping down the mines, you get some they have the gift of dousing with wires, but they will respond to anyone. One held a rod two metres long with a bit of opal in the end of it as he waved it around over the ground, while his mate looked on in admiration of his gift. Waving it around in the dust while another miner, shouting "Bluey, you won't catch any fish over there!" One day an official looking couple, two officers, said they were looking for a man that has escaped from the lunatic asylum. He has gone off his head, I thought, about working in the blazing sun, being bitten to death by flies in the day and mosquitos during the night and sleeping with bundles of gelignite under the bed and snakes dropping down the shafts and said officer, arrest the first man you come across. Living off rabbit and prickly pear is a hard struggle. One day Billy came into our camp. He struck a patch of opal, a workmate that we had been sharing a claim with, did love his ale. He used to sing, the pub with no beer. His grandad was an Afghan camel driver, one day he told us while dying for a beef has walked seven miles into town to sell a few cheap opals and have a drink. As he started back the heavens opened, so he walked into the local police station and as no one was there he got into a cell and got his head down. The local drunk in the next cell called the cop to tell him of the squatter, the sergeant said stop lying to me until he looked into the next cell and said "What are you bloody doing in there?" Lex said, "Well it was raining last night." To which the cop replied, "You better fuck off before I turn the key then!!" Another bunch of Hells Angels roared up on their bikes. It was a bit of a scorcher, at 38 degrees and when they saw the free open air swimming pool, two of them flung off their leathers and dived in. There was a problem – the water was drawn from the Artesian Basin, 3000 feet below, and came up hot, so they still hold the record for two seconds in and out. One successful miner that hit it rich had a boring machine, and for a joke, sank a shaft, the opal level about 50 feet down and salted the spoiler heap with good looking opal chippings. Miners are always looking out for new good ground to mine. Once they saw the good-looking chippings, they immediately stake their claim, and it started a rush on banging pegs in and digging like mad. We knew a family from the UK, The Smiths. They had three ginger haired sons, and they were down about 20 feet, while the sick joker was in the Digger's Rest with his mate drinking cold beers and laughing their heads off.

One day lunatic Billy, as we called him, said he had struck a patch of opal and "am inviting you and your brother and Lex out for a night on the booze. There is a nice little watering hole about 30 miles away. I got another couple of mates to go along as well". Lex said, wow a free night on the booze. I said watch what you are getting yourselves into. He is totally unstable at the best of times. To be tanked up with a 30-mile dirt pot-holed road with big dips in it where dry creeks had gone through, you fly through the air when coming out of one, and full of booze at 70 mile per hour, I declined to go on the grounds of sanity. At, midday they both came to our camp, blood spattered on his shirt, and beard. "That facking lunatic, driving like a bat out of hell, screaming at him slow down, he finally screeched to a halt in a cloud of dust. We could hardly land a blow on each other through the dust and the booze, so we got back in the car, there is nothing like an Aussie get together is there?

So, after eight months of sun, snakes and mosquitos and living off rabbit and prickly pear, it was time to head back to the bright lights of Sydney. With the building boom on and loads of trowels work!! DAMN! Well at least a trade puts food on the table so me and my younger brother got stuck in for the next 12 months. He never took to it, the heat and the whole Aussie attitude. Plus, they were calling young men up for Vietnam at the time. Most people don't realise that POMEs also were in Vietnam as they were called up, who went to put their lives at risk for another unpopular war, as it turned out, a disaster as all wars are. Well, back to the UK with trowel in hand still buzzing for adventure on wide opens plains, beats shoving crap up a wall in a Brummie cupboard. Some years after our return, my other brother, George, had gone to live in South Africa, and still being single, apart from a couple of romances, I booked a flight, the exchange rate was good. I had in the past ten years, renovated two old houses and built one. So, as the plane was landing in Johannesburg, you could see loads of blue patches everywhere, they turned out to be swimming pools. I thought it was a beautiful country, all well managed, grass outside instead of pavements. As a lover of nature, I found the bird life to be fantastic. Brilliant red cardinals and yellow ones. There was a tailer bird, whose tail was three times longer than its body. Endless others. There was a well-established ex-pat community and there would be a BBQ practically every weekend at different friends' houses. The cost of living was very cheap in comparison to the UK. Apart from the international condemnation from the international press about apartheid, I found the black Africans, those that worked in the communities were happy and friendly and a much better attitude than you get in the community than that you get in the UK. I don't want to get political, but I think that the Afrikaner are a handsome race, the men are well built, and the women are fine looking.

The word Apartheid is condemned by the West, but it merely means "separate communities". Fast forward to today and many who experienced this multi-racial mix would choose to live amongst mostly white suburbs. The suburbs were mostly litter free and well-manicured lawns, in the 80s the paddy wagons would patrol the suburbs after 6pm and any black men hanging around white communities would be driven back to their townships. I know many would find this a shocking racial act. Well, the protests it came to pass and the result, the crime went through the roof. To look outside your house at 10pm and see half a dozen black men outside your gate was unsettling. Yes, it is hard for them but such a large population, many are flooded in from surrounding country and compete with the locals for jobs. Well apartheid still exists but it is the opposite way around now. Political leaders are black, living in wealth while the native people live in poverty and of course there are very few ex-pats left, as their jobs were replaced by the Black population. Just to wind back a little, all of my life, I have what I call some psychic experiences which I will elaborate on later in this book. So, while I was in Jo-burg, I called into a spiritualised church, I am more curious about it than taking it all in. I say some mediums cannot read a gas meter. Just to prove how dangerous the country was becoming; I spoke to the medium after the service. I noticed a leather strap inside his coat for a gun holster. He said yes, that is how the country is going, you have to protect yourself. A year later, after the church service, his son and himself got out of the car in the drive and two black men shot and wounded them both. They took off with his car. So, an engineer, invented a powerful spring-loaded metal arm, fixed under the driver's side because of the car jacking at traffic lights. It was selling well but the government banned it for breaking too may legs. Well, that country might be beautiful, but it is not for me. I felt much safer down under. So, off to Aussie again. I got a friend who was a cooper in the UK in Wolverhampton had spent years training for that career, but when metal barrels replaced wooden beer barrels, every cooper in the country lost his job. The workshop of the world and the sell-out continues. Well, Bob was in what was called the Vincent motorbike club, it was an international affair, he had the second original bike made, worth a few bob. A group of them would take off every Sunday for a drive out. He also, like me, had a love for nature and animals. He had planted lots of fruit trees in his garden and started a job at a large vineyard, in the Barossa Valley, Adelaide, as a cooper. He could get port in a 20-litre container, dirt cheap. I loved it and made a lot of friends from parts of the UK, there seemed to be a few from Yorkshire, one guy was an ex-jockey named Tony. He took a job way out in the bush on the rabbit fence, he had to live there for a while. He said the heat was a killer and about 3.30pm a wind would pick up and all the men would shout the Doctor had arrived. I did a bit of renovation on his house. His daughter also engaged me with some work on her house. What a nice house, swimming pool and tennis court. She was separated from her husband, and she has a bit of a reputation you might say. One day while cooling off in the pool with her two children, she came down the steps of her house in her dressing gown, as bold as brass she showed her ass by slipping it off and dropping into the pool. I still did not lower my prices. What a character; she did not give a damn and loved being at the outdoor market, selling bric-a-brac, livestock etc. She loved to yell really loud, here, if bidding, and laugh. One day a guy was looking at a box of soap, she said, "Buy it…you bloody need it." Her dad said she shows me up. When she suspected her husband of flirting with a woman in the house, she hid behind the sofa with a shotgun as it was a big room. She waited for the conversation to get hot, when just as clothes were about to be removed she jumped out from behind the sofa, he yelled "Sally!" The look on his face. He said, "Now, Sallym don't be silly put it down, please put it down!" Her mother said to her later you should have waited for him to show his arse and then jump out!!

Another guy I met was another Yorkshireman, his wife's maiden name was Quinn, a descendant of Ned Kelly's, on his mother's side. Dennis was a proper Yorkshireman, he would stop his truck along the roadside, if he saw a few beer cans and say, "There is five cents on them". I swear he always stood near the doorway of a meeting in case there was a collection tin coming around. He had a small farm with pigs, sheep and chooks, but worked as a cook on a oil rig at sea, six weeks on and six weeks off, while his wife Margaret looked after the livestock. I bought a farmhouse on 40 acres called Stone Field. That describes the landscape. It had two and half stumpies (lizards) per acre. I was never so pleased, huge horizons, nothing but wheat and wool paddocks surrounded for miles. No water, just water tanks on the corner of the houses and sheds. A big house, the lounge and kitchen were 40 square yards. I got on well with the neighbours about two miles up the road. All dirt roads, they were mainly all Lutherans who had come over and settled in the 19th Century from Germany. They had established themselves in the wine industry, like Wolf Blass and Penfolds. I loved the big wide-open roads; I could drive to the Gawler market about 40 miles in less than 40 minutes. I got a bit established doing building work on farms. The word got around; I think that the Lutherans are some of the nicest folks I had met. They were religious and attended church, the children seemed well-behaved. While working on a job they would sit me down for a meal. I remember being invited to a big get together, outdoor picnic, they came from miles, met in a lovely spot. I bet there was a gathering of 80 or more, reminded me of the film, Oklahoma, children played their musical instruments and quizzes being played and plenty of booze. Neil on the next farm to me, had three daughters, pretty girls, but the youngest one was a real beauty. I reckon she would have won an Australian beauty contest. The odd one out was a real outback Sheila, not a Lutheran, more of a ring barker, a real jackaroo. She said I got stopped on a dirt road for a breathalyser, by a young pup of a cop. He said blow into here, she said you're after a blow job, are ya? He went as red as a turkey cock's arse. The local work was drying up and I was travelling 200-mile round trip for a month, I had got some livestock as I always wanted. The farmer who farms the local paddocks, 500 acres at a time, John Schmitt, a very German sounding name, his son Mark, worked from dawn 'til dusk, he said to me one day, "Mick, all my life consists of is wheat and wool, right from a child. Don't anyone kid you that farming is easy; it is bloody hard". Well, I ran out of work. I finished Mark's house repairs; we are looking for a man who could stand in for someone who has left. They owned and ran 6,000 acres and now it is burn off time. Miles of tumbleweed covered the paddocks this time of the year. I run the machine over, cutting and heaping it together. After a couple of days, you follow me with a flame thrower. I strapped this tank of petrol on my back and was shown the ropes. A six-foot flame blasted out, he said get the wind behind you. I said, "You bet I will!" This went on for about a week until I noticed a bit of flame coming out of a crack in the tube – that ended my experience. It was almost finished anyway.

I had now established a menagerie of animals, ducks, chooks, a sow and a litter. I noticed flocks of parrots and galahs – hundreds of them, sulphur crested cockatoos. They can do a lot of damage to the wheat and hang on the stalks so the husk drops to the ground; there were also goshawks flying overhead that would snatch pigeons and other birds. I know they look splendid but ruthless ripping chunks out of live birds. One day I saw what looked like a branch that moved in the bush, it turned out to be a family of tawny frog mouths. Then one day all the ducks and chooks froze still, I thought the hawks are back. I crept down in between the sheds and saw nothing, then I realised what it was. I was about one stride away from a two-metre-long brown snake. But don't bother them and they go on their way. I could go a whole week without seeing anyone. That suited me, better than being on the M6 in the UK. Then one day I saw the tell-tale dust of a vehicle coming down my track, it was two vehicles, stopped in a cloud of dust and four men jumped out of a van and a car. Two rushed over to the sheds and two to the house. "Police," they shouted. "Drugs squad," showing me his ID card. "What do you want here?" I asked. We heard you have a crop growing. "Yes," I replied. "There." I pointed to a patch of broad beans in the garden. No, he said and made his way into every room in the house. Well, I said, it seems like someone has sent you on a fool's errand. They climbed back into their vehicles, not even a word of apology, they would have got the sharp end of my tongue. I do have a temper, only when I am pushed. But my boxing skill was no good against four. You see the guy an Italian who used to own the place, used to grow the stuff, I was told, he threw 200 plants down the old well and his mate took the rap and left the State. I am in the middle of nowhere minding my own business on a Sunday morning sitting outside, not a soul about, then suddenly I hear voices. I know I explained in this book, that I have a certain psychic gift, so these voices, I am trying to strain to get a message. I must relax and send out my thoughts, five minutes and nothing, then I just happened to look above my head to see a large barrage ballon with four people looking down at me. You can't make it up. I am in the middle of nowhere and being spied on from above, a guy shouted, we are on a balloon trip and are coming down, can we land on your paddock?

The last job I did whilst down under was a large straw bailed house, with a classroom inside as some folk had a distance to travel to school and kept them at home for their lessons. During harvest time young boys from 12 years upwards would be off school which was overlooked because what follows for them is working with wheat and wool. I sweated on that straw baled house. It was the last big job on the trowel. It took 20 tonnes of sand and cement; I had just gone 60 years of age and still using the tool of torture – well, it puts tucker on the plate.

My Psychic Dreams.

I don't think there are many living that sometimes question when we pass over this mortal coil, that there may be a form of spiritual communication with endless populations, for thousands of years humans have believed in a God-like overseer, in a celestial heaven. As far as man-made religions are concerned, I am an atheist. Like me, you are also an atheist if you only believe in one God and dismiss the 990 others, so now to put my serious cap on, I have sampled more than my fair share of life's experiences. I felt that this subject I am about to write will be of interest to others. I have read a few books, one brilliant author and scientist, Richard Dawkins, states that the obvious proof he elaborated on is the progress of evolution and makes a scientific observation that once the brain rots away there is no possible channel of any form of spiritual communication. While I am fully in agreement of his scientific proof, I believe that by my own experiences, there is a form of communication that survives somehow beyond death. A form of telepathy, to me there is no doubt that we are spiritual as well as a physical being. I will elaborate on my experience of astral flight. I rose from the bed, as I am also gifted with recording most of my dreams, but this was not a dream. I thought, be calm and go with it. I drifted towards the door; it connected to the upstairs landing and a door right opposite. I went straight through both doors, across the back bedroom and towards the sash window and went straight through, thinking this is incredible. I saw the night sky and rose above the roof, looking over at the streetlights. I thought I have always wondered about life on other planets so my thoughts were to rise up into the sky, to prove that I am in a spirit form, I would test it and go into next door neighbour's bedroom and tell him the next day, exactly what he has in his bedroom. As I went towards the window, the next moment, I was under a blue sky floating over a red sandstone landscape and going over a huge cliff, the shock brought me back and onto my bed. When I spoke to Mrs Berry, a top medium, she said stop, you didn't go through the window. Spirits will not allow you to use them for self-gain. I know the difference between dreaming and a conscious mind and true psychic dreams, meaning the event follows the next day or later. One thing seems I am contradicting my above statement, not for self-gain but I have done a few good deeds for free in my life. I will elaborate further in this book. After retiring, I started to have a bet on the horses. Now this is something that a punter would dream of. Given a Grand National winner and a Gold Cup winner. I did not back the Grand National winner. I saw my younger brother who had passed over with money in his hand and laughing. Then I saw a medium; this medium would very often say, you must read the philosophy of a red Indian guide, called Silver Birch. It did pass my mind, even though I did not back it, it won at 33-1. So, when Gold Cup Day arrived, I had an amusing thought – come on, give us a tip. What I saw in a dream was my younger brother and an old school mate named Davies, Paul my brother was sitting on a fence with money in his hand. Then he fell over the fence, towards the final fence, the almost unbeatable horse Kato Star hit the fence and fell over the fence, and Imperial Commander won the race. Owned by Nigel Christian Davies. I had a good win.

Spiritual churches, I am sometimes sceptical of what I have witnessed. I speak plainly and say with most of them put on a show and draw out the naïve what fits their expectations. But I think some could not read a gas meter as a lot of them are in it for the money or fancy themselves as a performer, but occasionally there are some genuinely gifted mediums. Scientists say this is an impossibility. As I have said, I am a big fan of Richard Dawkins, the scientist and atheist. As they say once the brain decomposes there can be no form of communication. But I go beyond that, by what I have experienced. There is a form of spiritual communication.

I have seen much in my psychic dreams, I spent some time in South Africa and stayed what was called house sitting, looking after a house while the owner was away for a week. One morning just coming to, in bed, not quite awake, I looked up and saw water running through a light ceiling fitting. At that a big strapping guy stood up, in a black vest, holding a towel to his head, I thought "That was a strange vision". And asked the neighbour about the previous tenant and did he know anything about him; he said yes, he had heard he had climbed on the roof to check a leak and fell off. I said did he die due to the fall; he said he didn't know but said he was related to a South African heavyweight boxing champion, I believed in the 1980s. Maybe some out there reading this knows.

Also, a child went missing and I asked for help in a dream, I was going through a field with the corn stalks brushing my face. The little girl was found in a pool, amongst stalks of bullrushes. On another occasion, I dreamt of my brother-in-law who had been separated from my sister for many years. He was in his car by the sea. The water was rushing in. When I enquired with my sister, she said, his body was found in the sea – he had committed suicide by drowning.

The one thing I was gifted with is healing, two mediums with a good reputation told me so. I never got involved with this in spiritualist churches, I was never a member; in fact, I was a critic at times. I am not easily convinced. I am a free spirit by nature, so over the years, I would lay my healing hands on family and friends, and love to hear a sceptic say, no kidding that has relieved my pain!

What is important is that it is all freely given. I could go on about a variety of conditions that have benefited from my healing. What readers might think now, is, I am cooking up this story. A young attractive woman I met with a little girl, she looked so slim, her name was Susan. She told me that she had anorexia. She allowed me to administer healing by laying my hands on her. As I do, we had a joke, then something happened to me that I have never experienced before. I lay in bed one morning and a woman spoke to me, she said, Susan has been ill for quite some time now. She is a nice girl, but she is getting over it. For about eight years and you did it. At that a noise in the background brought that encounter to an end. A month later, I spoke to Sue and asked how are you. She said she felt much better and had put a couple of pounds on and "an inch on my bust". I asked her how long she had been ill for. She said about eight years. I had a bit of a reputation and saw quite a few folks; the heartbreak is always terminally ill children, which I saw three of. What would you not give to save a child? I was asked to call and see a little girl with terminal cancer, her name was Stephanie Chapman, from Short Heath, West Midlands. I met her parents, Steve and Rose, I said I hope she responds to get some relief, which she did. Of course, you have to be realistic, I think that with certain people like me, as a healing energy that transfers to the sick and helps to put in motion a healing energy to the patient, like a jump lead. I recall the happiness on that pretty little girl's face, Stephanie Chapman, when she represented Birmingham's Children's Hospice and met Kylie Minogue and Princess Diana. She said to the Princess, "I'm going to be a bridesmaid next month." "Oh, that is lovely," said the Princess, "who to?" Oh my mother's wedding. Rose said, "I went quite red". That was in the 1980s. Why I write this is because they are facts to prove to anyone of my character. I think there is nothing crueller to a mother than losing a child. Sadly, Stephanie passed away. Finally, I refer to a most compelling psychic dream about the missing child Madeleine McCann, who disappeared in May 2007. It was such a shocking case for the parents. Two nights after she had not been found, as I once asked for help in my mind, there does exist a power beyond our consciousness. What motivated me to ask was the dream I had had with the previous missing child. In this case, I was shown three scenes, the first scene I was in a room looking into another room and a child being struck by a man twice and lying motionless on the floor. The next I was travelling along the road and in between some houses down an incline of a dirt track, then turned left into a yard like a small parking area. There I saw a small concrete loading deck with a 40 gallon drum on it, which reminded me of a place I used to work in, youth and animal parts disposal place. The most important part was the next scene of a young couple in their 30s in handcuffs. She has long fair hair and strangely she was cursing the man she was with, in either a German or Dutch accent. It was not for a few years later that I heard that a man was questioned twice by the police that ran a pet crematorium business, that had been previously jailed in Holland for murder. His fitted the animal disposal business I dreamt. I wondered if the child's body was cremated there. But the owner stated the business had closed before the child went missing. It was in May 2007 I reported to the Walsall West Midlands Police, a WPC attended the desk. I thought she may think I am an attention-seeking headcase. But no, she said it is OK, I will take your statement. I explained to her all that I have written down and she photocopied my statement, saying here is a copy for you and one for me. She would have been about 40 years of age, at the time, and if is correct she signed her name as "Jones". I must admit that I had put that dream to rest, until a few years ago, I heard a young German man had been arrested as the suspect. I also saw a German woman in the dream, which only came out in the news, later. I questioned why in the dream she was cursing him. Did she realise or think, that Bruckner had killed the child? The animal disposal yard that was put down in my statement came to light in some degree when I heard of a man being questioned twice who ran a pet crematorium. To my great annoyance, my photocopied statement was accidently disposed of with some old papers. So, I wrote to the police data protection department, after pursuing the police copy with no luck finding and it coming to light that they had searched for it using an incorrect Christian name. So, I wrote again; the reply was we have gone through all the files, three times now and nothing you have requested can be found. I even managed to fund a further search to locate the WPC named Jones, or the statement copy. It seems after a certain time some statements are disposed of. I even went to Bloxwich police statement as the staff of Walsall had all been relocated there after it was demolished. But all I got was no information can be divulged to the public about the staff. I would have hoped it was possible that WPC Jones the desk duty sergeant, was still stationed there and perhaps put my statement in another secure file. Can anyone working at the police HQ in May 2007 recall a desk attendant named Jones and could you please send a message via email to michaelmcnally746@gmail.com

I can finally add that even if my statement is found, nothing can change the circumstances. I do believe Bruckner is guilty.

Other Psychic Encounters

My younger sister Josie had passed away and I lit a candle for her and thought about her life, quietly until the candle burnt out. I looked at the wax that remained in the saucer, it had five flat circular shapes and a circle in the middle where the candle had stood. It was a flower, a long run off like a stalk. I took a photo with me, and a woman who had psychic ability said to me a woman in spirit has given you a flower. I sent the photo to someone who had spiritual beliefs, in signs by the results of candles melting. It was never returned back, it is out there somewhere, so please send it back if you are reading this. Email above.

On another occasion I was sending out what is called absent healing to a young woman who had sadly passed away, then one night in bed, I sensed two women standing by my bedside, one said I have come to thank you for trying to help. I smiled as I have a sense of humour, and I pulled the sheets back and said jump in. I heard some chuckling going on and Iris said I have got to go now; at that I physically jumped as a cold hand was put on my bare chest.

So, I will close now. I hope this book has given you a good laugh. Of course, my more serious side of psychic dreams. I am a comedy scribbler not an author, at 82 years old, as old as a conker tree, and just running on two pistons, I should be pushing the daisies up now, so to speak. If it was not for the NHS who saved me, I have a scar three inches below my navel right up to my neck to prove it. Oh, and a metal ankle put in last winter due to a fall, my foot was swinging loose, ambulance time was 12 hours, so I wrapped it up with masking tape, and done a Clint Eastwood on it with a few tots of whiskey. I said to a pretty nurse who attended me, you have left me with a big hard on. She blushed a little. I said, "No, no, from my ankle to my knee in plaster!" and she chuckled. I can't help myself, can I?

Could anyone who has read this and can authenticate my stories email me on the email above.

Best wishes
Michael.

Humorous Poems

"The Byelection"

There is a byelection coming I bet you can't wait, they'm
all kissin' babbies and hangin' around the gate. You have
got red ones and blues ones and some in between, there are
nutters to strutters and a gay sequinned Queen. They run
up and down and plaster the street with leaflets of promises
they really can't meet. And rosettes are whoppers I ain't
kiddin' our kid and cover the size of a dustbin lid.

An extremist whose Volkswagen had just broken down
said all I need is a putsch to take over the town. They shake
the red flag and think you are fickle because on tother side
is a hammer and sickle. A Tory with a story blamed it on
the world recession, he should drop on his knees and go to
confession. The Liberals say motorways, it's all to console ya,
because they they are using Big Cyril on the road for a roller.
You got left wing and right wing, the Centre and the top,
there is more wings in politics than a Kentucky Fried Shop!

And politicians bright, there was one from Wigan, who
thought a Left-wing coup was a wounded pigeon. Now you
Black Country folk love a loff and a joke and sometimes
a slap and a tickle. I said what do you think cock of a
NATO block, she said I'd rather have a raspberry ripple. A
politician's head was used for spotting the brain but crosses

galore you could still not score, and your savings would go down the drain. They say we will clean up the dog turds and shift all the rubble but ten years hence with their dim sense and we will still be in bad trouble.

"The Hypochondriac"

Do you know a hypochondriac who just can't get no sleep? And swears lumbago is always on the creep. She has everything from chicken pox to a type of Zulu flu and if it is not in the medical book, she will swear it is something new.

She has had prickly heat, athletes' feet and a hot flush to a carbuncle a cancered ear, a blistered rear and an allergy off her uncle. If you had seen her kitchen, you would not believe your eyes, you would swear it was a chemist shop and I ain't tellin' no lies.

She got herbs and pills for all sorts of ills, snake venom to some lotion. Something strange brewed on the range to a bit of magic potion. She had a bout of gallstones and frightened her dear old spouse; cos she swore she had a bucket full and pebbled dashed a house.

With chilblains in her toes and the rickets made her lame, she had a tennis elbow and never played a game. There was rumour of a tumour, it was neither here or there, a polypus, a touch of thrush and a bout of diarrhoea. She

suffered with the gout, and it weren't through drinking
stout. And suffered Berry-berry and you'll never find
her merry.

She had a touch of croup and a problem
with the loop and I swear the way they
put it in it always made her stoop.

So they took her dear old ticker out and put in a
carburettor, she does 80 round the block
but she ain't getting' no better.

So God Bless her dear old heart for ailments
she's got plenty. I am buying a card you
can't be hard next week she is 120.

"Damn Music"

Music gorblimey they blast you, our kid. Dow, ya lugs take
a bashing when you're watchin' El Cid.

You put on the box it don't matter what's on, from Dallas,
The Callus and Steptoe and Son.

They will make you have it and you'll curse 'til you're hot
and you'll suffer all night 'til you see the last spot. They
blast you with sirens and violins for love and ministers of
angels that scream from above.

The heroes in danger or having a scrap, comes a deafening a crescendo like the Mother-in–Law's trap.

The noise is terrific, and your head starts to pound and you are hooked like an addict on an unbearable sound.

You got trumpets for strumpets and flutes and pianos and a sixty-piece band for your Starsky and Tanners. Sometimes it is tranquil, it is all done for effect, from a yelping Apache to a husband hen-pecked.

Now your Germans and Japs, have a real morbid tune, like a death march that's playing on a battered bassoon. And the Hollywood starts can't do a thing wrong, for a slanty eyed Chink they bang on a gong.

And pirates have sea-songs from Blackbeard to Morgan for a blood splattered Drac out comes the organ. So, at the end of the night when you stand up for "Lizzie", they'll blast you again!
By God are you dizzy.

"Placid Woman"

What would he give for a placid woman, that was cooking and baking and doing some humming. He would stagger back home in a bit of a state, and she would open her arms and say "Darling, you are late".

Now back to reality instead there's this woman,
By God what a temper. It is like meeting a
wolf with piles and distemper.

He said, "I'm sorry, me darling,
I'm late through the fog."

He said, "Have I a nice dinner?"
She said, "Go and ask the dog."

She curdled his home-brew with a look on his face and
he dropped a bloomer with his humour, and she coshed
him with a plaice. She followed up with cast-iron pan and
God the speed it landed, it had been brewing on the stove
some time and his back was truly branded. They had a
fight every week and a kid every year, you got to make up
and you can't blame the beer.

Boozed he had been, well what a drop to drink, but kids
were told to pee in the pot and fill it to the brink. He
staggered around the back, it seemed an ungodly hour and
looked up at the window and down came a golden shower.

She's always been wild right from a kid and sometimes you
can't blame her for the things that she did. And we always
knew when her belly was up because you would be dodging
a plate, a pot or a cup.

Them were the days. Kids what a struggle you had a boot
up the ass instead of a cuddle.

Discipline was hard and haircuts were free, and when the
shears came out, we was all up a tree.

Once in a while we went to the flickers, and it was six hail
Marys if you seen some knickers. Eleven babbies in a three
up and two down, no wonder she has a temper and no
wonder she wears a frown.

"Old-Fashioned Names"

Some names you never hear, and some do disappear as old-
fashioned names go out of style. The names you hear today
are they really here to stay because they are trendy and
sound well up the aisle?

They have changed the name of Dicky to a fancy name
of Ricky, and Cuthbert, Burt and Alf have gone out the
door, then there is Wilf to Ebenezer a dead cert of a teaser
and some it seems you'll never hear no more. Enoch, Jake
and Horace to the deadly name of Boris are bygone names
that echo of the past.

But Dustin, Lee and Wayne, they wow complain because
they know you'll bet your life they'll last.

If they name you after Dad, you are very often sad,
especially if you're chatting up a girl. Cause she will ask you
"What's your name?" and you'll drop your head in shame
because its Ogi and you're bound to fail.

Now the women are the same when it comes to name a
name 'cause they have suffered the same as all mankind.
Like Violet, Pansy, Daisy might sound a little crazy but
them pretty flowers perfume like our Rose.

And it seemed that when they called them some say they
should have stalled them, but it is thought that counts that
way I s'pose.

But of all the names I've heard some do sound absurd, the
most dreaded name of all should go to Granny.

Because if you was to take a look it's the worst one in the
book, the most dreaded name of all is poor old "Fanny".

"Knackermon Ned"

Perhaps you've smelt a few things off and things that
weren't too grand, but when it comes to Ned and his truck
load of dread, he'd clear a whole grandstand.

He got hunches, pounches, bungs and lungs and you knew
when he passed by. You could stand and wait and count to
eight and it'd hit you in the eye.

Clotted blood, feet and meat and bladders by the score.

Bins that moved around at night
with tapeworms four foot four.

A blown-up cow and a half green sow was joy and a
bonus prize, he got sixty pair of feet to declare and
bucket full of blood shot eyes. And maggots were a
fisherman's dream and fill their eyes with mirth. But
there was a puzzle and wore muzzle and were six inches
around the girth.

Now Vera was a buxom lass and pulled pig's runners by the
mile, she stood proud in her wellies, knees in cows jellies
and gave him a toothless smile. Cos Vera was a two-timer
as most girls of today and had a loff with Tim the Toff
down the butcher's alleyway. Now, Ned was frantic, and
they stepped out in the yard as punches were the weapons
Ned chose one big and hard.

They slashed and bashed each other until droppings fell
like rain. Then he used a pair of bull's bells as a bolus and
tripped him by the drain.

He pelted him with faggots and whipped
him with a tail and rammed on his head
a farthing and his breath began to fail.

Now Vera and Ned got wed and the incense
filled the aisle, the service was read in record
time, and the priest had lost his smile.

Now if you girls are throwing up and this
sounds a big disgrace, remember when it's
melted down it is put upon your face.

"The Nosey Neighbour"

Have you got a nosey neighbour that does not miss a trick? If a car pulls up or a door is knocked she is out like lightning quick.

Her broom is carried on her arm as she marches up and down. That is the century on the entry and knows every tale in town.

She's got one red eye and that's no lie, through peeping through a crack. Behind the lace, her favourite place be it up the front or back.

She chatters to the milkman for rumours good or bad, for scandals, bills, sex or ills and make it twice as bad.

She knows what you had for breakfast and the colour of your suite and before your colour telly arrived it would be up and down the street.

And doing alterations, her brain must do a skip because you will always find her searching for clues within the skip.

If your MOT is faded and you don't display your tax, she'd be out there with a notebook and a biro out her slacks.

I thought of painting over her windows as you know we ain't all twerps but before I got me brushes out, she was out there with the turps.

Then I bought a bit of crumpet back as we were practising to elope then at half past two, I went to the loo and up come a periscope. That has really done it and I've gone right off my head. I am now living in a lovely home and guess who is in the next bed.

"Building Site Mates"

If ever you work the building sites, the characters you meet.

There is Doug the Chip and Chris the Lip and Ecca with his flyers and Ray would stay for extra pay and search for tat and wires. Now Bernie was a scaffolder, he was really quick and able, he wore his spanners on his belt and was lightning on a gable.

Archie was a brickie, and we really feared to follow him, he'd have played at Wembley so they say but then the army collared him.

We know that nobody's perfect and his walls ain't all a treat but I swear the way he handled that ball, he'd have laid them better with his feet,

Now Percy was a swearer, by God how he could cuss, the day a wasp stung his ass you should have heard the fuss.

Now catcher the truck at half past seven, you sat on a cold plank it were quite heaven. You'd freeze in the winter and

sweated in summer. The pipe had stuck to
me hands shouted Albert the plumber.

The worst winter of all was '63. Dogs stuck
to a post whilst having a pee.

The dole queue stretched out right round the block,
some walked straight in, it came as a shock. Outraged
we were and just would not buy it, a rope was suggested,
there was nearly a riot. Thank God for the spring
with no ice on the pond, remembering old mates with
memories so fond.

We followed rough brickies some were real rotters with
bow-legged walls and covered in snotters. So we plastered
and sweated to put things right, working like donkeys on
the old building site.

"Super-Hod"

The beams of the sun crept over the site as two figures
emerged in the first morning light.

The show-down was rumoured and long overdue for the
Tipton Tornado and Super-Hod from Crewe.

His hod was enormous and used for a shed, you could see
how he basted by the size of his head, the sides were like

ski-slopes and as tall as a man at the back, he never stopped
to speak a word, just left a smoky track.

The Tornado drawn out his pearl handle trowel and sparks
were sent flying in an almighty growl. Super-Hod's legs
like pistons and blares, worn out a shovel and burnt up the
stairs, the Tornado kept spreading no mercy had he, he'd
seen off six labourers before morning tea.

Float, skim or render, pebble dash or screed he often
challenged 20 men and gave them half a lead. Brought
up on cow-hair and lathes so they say and scratch-coated
six foremen who got in his way. Mean as a bull-ant and a
wanted man at that, his tax was due in Brum and Crewe,
Dumfries and Ballarat.

A bungalow done for breakfast and a two-bed flat for tea,
no donkey with a bionic hod will make a fool of he.

His crutch was now bleeding, he was so
red and sore, he went down slow like a
bag of dough in a pile up on the floor.

Get up, the Tornado snorted and kicked him where he lay,
you've only mixed up 40 tonnes, it ain't that time of day.

So, if you want to be a Super-Hod remember through and
through, the man with the scowl and the pearl handled
trowel, has notched up forty-two.

"The Pop Star"

Don't let him be a pop star let him grow up like a mon!

With purple hair and tinsel there and tonnes
of make-up on.

They shout and scream like a nightmare dream as certified
x-rater and the end of every song you need a good
translator.

If you are gay you're on your way even if your voice is lousy
because the director's dog got lost in the fog and called out
"Bousy-wousy".

Elton John, there's the one, Rod Stewart to Gary Glitter,
they shake and swing their hips around then off to the bank
they titter.

Zowie Bowie, Boy George and Marilyn
makes you wince, they frightened my poor
old moggie and I've never seen it since.

No wonder they made Marty Wilde and Adam's lost his
Faith. The Everly Brothers and some of the others would
never give them space.

The boots they wear are two feet high
and the colours make them twitch.

Some look like a pretty butterfly
and some a crimson witch.

The songs they sing are mainly love and done 20 years
before. They change the tune and drop a word, and you'll
bet it will be in the top score.

Still, it is better than working down the pit, and given the
chance you'd try it, because when you are known you're a
king on a throne and no matter how bad, they'll buy it.

"Enoch's Elderado"

He stumbled up a dusty track with pick and shovel on his
back and dreamt of treasures oh so grand across that harsh
and endless land.

A city boy by birth and right had stopped to settle for the
night. The deadly swarms he had not met was a three-
course meal for the vampire set.

They dived down low and took a taste, and
dive bombed him in hungry haste, they bit him in the
earhole and other holes as well, he scratched
himself raw, my God how he did swell.

You got stingers on wingers and snappers and clingers, if
you swat 'em or smack 'em they go for your fingers.

A cloud of flying Nashers a multitude of types, some with red and with green and some with fancy stripes. His cries were heard across the bush and agony were his howls, they dived down low to when he should go to exercise his bowels.

The years flew by like seconds, and he thought of his over-sexed wife, but he'd never had so many love bites in the whole of his married life.

So, he took off up that dusty track, with no pick and shovel on his back. He headed for a billabong; his strides were fast and very long. The shafts he sank were hard and deep, he said to hell with the gold, it'll have to keep.

"The worst Aussie Talent Show on Earth"

Looking back a while, whilst living Down Under was the worst talent show by far by thunder.

The chief of the panel was a spit for Les Patterson, with his hand on the buzzer for the act to come on. A singer came on and the buzzers went off, the chief of the panel started to scoff.

You are howling and growling and really no good and I would give you minus 10 if I could.

The singer got angry and wanted to fight, and told him to
stick his bananas where there ain't no light.

The one balled juggler fascinated us all, he got a loud
buzzer for dropping the ball.

Then the ventriloquist Santa made us all loff. He tripped
on the stage and his beard fell off.

A yodeller came on in a black aqualung and passed out
before finishing the song that he sung.

Then came a real Ausssie that painted the bridge, some say
he was born in a place called the ridge.

He said you can shove all your points, and we cheered with
glee and we know him today as "Crocodile Dundee".

"The Dream-Home"

I'm going to build a dream home for the Mrs and me. There
is a bosting plot being standing by the old oak tree.

Permission must be granted and you must
submit your plans and take it to the town
hall and leave it in their hands.

I paid a fee for the picture, and he drew a pretty house, the
price was not bad as some of them had shocked the spouse.

Six months seem to come and go and a
letter said you've won. Go and draw a
mortgage up, you've started all the fun.

The manager looked me up and down and
eyed me with a glare. He said, "Do you owe
any money out, I got to start somewhere."

Married, single or in between this gave me some surprise, a
car a mortgage or TV I do not want any lies.

I bost his grip from me throat and thought is the friendly
bank, I said I respect your approach dear manager but do
you have to be so frank.

I made a start, the footings in. A chap said do you want to
make a draw. He said I charge a fee don't blame me; I'm
coming six times more.

Professional fees you are on your knees just like a battered
ball, you are sent around in circles it drives you up the
wall. The inspector was keen as mustard I mean and would
not budge an inch from his station. The one thing that he
passed and that wouldn't last was rock hard constipation.

The house was nearly finished, and he measured every
room, I was happy at seven feet five in height but an inch
short, this spelt doom.

MICK MCNALLY

You'll have to jack it up he said and take off
all the roof. But you could have a two-inch
carpet laid for God's strewth.

"My Psychic Dream"

I had a psychic dream so please be aware I hear
voices and sounds when nobody's there.

Is the wind or is it the rain or the nosey neighbour that has
kicked off again.

Sometimes they are happy and sometimes they are
sad. I've always had them since I was a lad.

I have seen beautiful images, all kinds of things, from wild-
flower meadows to bright angels' wings.

Sometimes they are scary this I can swear, so if I get a
bowel movement, please be aware.

One night I floated off the bed, I thought I was going off
my head, straight through the door even though it was
locked. I drifted outside fascinated not shocked.

As I drifted outside viewing the sites, a voice
boomed out "Get back, no light".

So, off to the spiritualist church to enquire, why I see
mountainous waves and volcanic fire.

"You are psychic, my lad, don't blame the booze, keep
welcoming spirits in sleep when you snooze."

I don't mind the good ones when given a winner and spend
all the money. Does that make me a sinner?

"A Black Country Mon"

He hammered all day in the heat and the smoke, that was
the days of the Black Country folk. His eldest son fancies
his chances, he preferred to be scrapping in the street than
going to dances.

"Lend us a tanner, Dad, to join a boxing club."

He said, "OK, my lad, but it is only a sub!"

Back from his venture the evidence was clear, black eye, red
nose and cauliflower ear.

He said, "My lad, I don't think you've won!"

But by the look on your face, you've had
your money's worth, son!

MICK MCNALLY

"The Last Song Thrush"

He sings on high from rooftop, chimney and a bush and builds a nest in hawthorn a bowl of mud, the Thrush.

Protected by those deadly thorns to keep predators at bay. Now, the skies are filled with Raptors, the Magpie and the Jay.

No bird was more common, they inhabited every street, and you could hear their song on high, a melody so sweet.

No more Thrushes' anvils, scattered with broken shells, a gardener's friend they called him from the meadows to the dells. Now pesticides deprive him, no snails his favourite food, with hedgerows ripped out by the mile nowhere to rear his brood.

It seems they've gone forever; it makes your memory sag. The only way you'll see one now is on the Baggies' flag.

Now, Two Limericks For The Kids

"The Musical Newt"

Nigel was a nuisance and a musical newt. He had a drum and a fiddle and a rusty old flute.

He blew and he blew until his cheeks were red, then hammered on his drum until it hurt his head. What a noise what a din, he was heading for the charts, and dragonflies on lily pads took off just like darts.

He played to the blackbird the linnet and the lark.

But within half an hour he'd emptied all the park.

I must start a fan club they really are so fond.

The frogs saw him coming and they dived back in the pond.

I really need a manager to put me on the road, his old pal Tom said sign right here, he was a half-deaf toad.

He had a black and yellow waistcoat and a really fancy crest. I will get to number one, he said, I am better than the rest.

He finally got an audition like he really knew he could, so he blasted a tune in the middle of June, and they all dived beneath the mud.

"Colour Prejudice"

Deep in the countryside with colours all aglow. Red, pink, blue and orange with all the world to show. The cornflower shook her head and looked towards the sky and said I am the best of all how could anyone deny.

Rosy red and orange, splendid colour of the rose, said I am the best of all and this I do propose.

Yellow shone the sunflower to the golden daffodil, a meadow of buttercups for all the world to thrill.

Can I join in a voice called out, he was so dark and grey. They laughed at his colour and sent him on his way.

But on and on the blue, blue sky could not block out the sun.

And all around on the ground the dying had begun.

The wise old owl was sent for, he did not give a hoot.

When he told them of their meanness when they gave Mr Grey the boot.

He said the compost in the muckheap, is not pretty
blue or pink, but encourages you to grow even though it
might stink.

Then up spoke the rainbow, no colour could compare, said
it is he who gave you life you must all be aware

Then a rumble of loud thunder from behind a distant hill.

The breeze shook the trees where once they stood so still.
Then a colour came, not pretty but shades of darkest grey
and sprinkled silver raindrops that came to save the day.

So, remember with your colours and some are very plain,
we must all contribute to life, that is all I can explain.